Finding Beauty in Midst of your Pain

Finding Beauty in Midst of your Pain

Felicia Scott

I greet you in the precious name of our Lord and Savior Jesus Christ. In Matthew 22:37 Jesus says: thou shalt love the Lord thy God with all thy heart, and with all thy soul, and with all thy mind. He says this is the first and great commandment. He goes on to say the second is like unto it, thou shalt love thy neighbor as thyself.

I want to encourage you to allow God to be first in your life. Nothing or no one should come before God. God loves us so much that He gave His only Son, Jesus, to die and save us from our sins. Through his death, we have the opportunity to have eternal life with Him in Glory. Every good thing that has ever happened to us is a Blessings from God.

And then I want to encourage you to show love to other people. Treat others the way you want to be treated. Treat them with love and respect.

And God will Bless you for it.

Rev. Dr. Ernest P. Scott Jr

"Broken"

Have you ever been broken? Broken does not mean only physical bones but sometimes we are broken mentally. Sometimes we have been mentally broken to the point where it seems like there is only one thing to do to get out of my misery but I'm here to tell you there is another way. There are times in our lives we allow people to see how strong we are on the outside but on the inside, we are screaming, "please help me," "I need help." Look at me I am a wreck about to happen, can't you read my eyes, can't you see I'm hurting inside, can't you see it behind my smile? A lot of times we are afraid to ask for help and we are too busy doing our own thing in order to help someone else.

God wants you to know that "He is here" for you. TRUST, and BELIEVE that God will see you through, because God said "I'm still here. You may have a lot of medical problems, no food to eat. You may even be sick and tired of being sick all the time, you may feel broken, but God said, "I'm still here." Through your heartache, pain, trials and tribulations, the loss of a job, the times that you didn't know where your next meal was coming from, the cycle of life when it seems like everything is going wrong and nothing seem to be going right for you, you may have been broken but God said, "I'm still here."

2 Corinthians 1:3-4:- Praise be to the God and Father who is full of mercy and all comfort. He comforts us every time we have trouble so when others have trouble, we can comfort them with the same comfort God has given us. God is telling you "I'm still here."

He is telling you in His word that you may be crushed, and you may feel broken, but He is still here. You may be lied on and feel like life is not worth living but He is still here. Things may not be going the way you want it, and you may feel neglected, but He is still here. He knows all that you are going through, and He has never left you but have been there watching and blessing you. We are a broken people looking for a quick fix, but God says; just keep praying and reach out because "I am still here" .

Praise God because you wear His name.

Rev. Dr. Sherleen B. Scott

"Forward"

Felicia Scott has done an amazing job of bringing the scriptures and message of the love of God to life in her writing. She intricately intertwines the reality of life's sufferings with the hope given in the bible. Her words are thrown out to the reader like a giant rope giving us a glimpse of the power of redemption, healing and Jesus saving grace. Felicia is able to communicate in a very real and down to earth way the victories she has experienced and challenges that she has overcome. Her book, *Finding Beauty In the Midst of Your Pain* clearly shows that she is not a novice to writing with many years of experience shining brightly through every line leaving the reader captivated. These life-giving nuggets in this book are literally acts of evangelism reaching out to lift the reader up in the beauty of the Lord. Felicia Scott's writing is truly a unique gift and treasure from God Almighty Himself.

Vanette Howard is the author of Prayer Changes Things and founder of Coffee & Girltalk with God Womens Group in Fort Worth, Texas.

Contents

"See The Vision"

If I were blind and could not see,
What is the vision designed for me?
Not by sight I believe is the best way to be,
When it comes to following your destiny.
For Faith and Vision goes hand in hand,
And with both you must believe.
It is the image of things hoped for
When it seems, all hope is gone.
A purpose designed by God is placed in our heart,
To help and show you just where to start.
Make the vision plain and let others see,
This is how God gets the glory,
And the people can start to believe
That God had laid the foundation before we were born,
He designed each of us to fight the war,
Preparing us for battle with every trial.
This is how we are getting strong,
But always remember to whom you belong.
There will be drama, chaos, heartache, pain and good days,
Nights will turn into days again
But always remember the vision stays the same.

"Life"

Broken spirit, broken souls,
Fear of the night, secrets untold.
But still, you rise to see another day,
Praying that the misery will soon go away,
You fight for respect, but no one understands,
How you remain in the Father's hands.
You have your own doubts and regrets,
But there is one thing you will never forget,
How you have been broken down so low
That up was the only way to go.
You have spent many nights crying on the inside,
Praying that the chaos would soon subside.
But you realize that this is only a test,
And you will soon come out better than the rest.
That day is not over it has just begun,
For there is still a race to be run.
Blood, sweat and tears the motivation needed,
To finish this thing called life.

"We Will Meet Again"

(In memory of Mama Peaches)

The world has left you with hurt and pain.
A constant night filled with rain.
But you still smiled every day,
Never letting the worries of this life get in your way.
The Lord is preparing you for something great,
Something that no man can take.
For God is about to sweep you off your feet,
Like your Boaz you are going to meet.
A queen with a crown, a heart of Gold,
Will surely be missed from this earthly home.
Taken where you will get your well-deserved rest.
Remembering God only takes the best.
No more sickness and no more tears,
In Heaven there will be nothing to fear.
Waiting and resting in your eternal home,
Watching for your loved one soon to come.
Again, together where we will meet,
Oh, how happy we will be.

"I'm Free"

Lord, you said that I am free to let go.
Free to live a beautiful life.
Free to have unspeakable joy inside.
Free to be who you called me to be.
Free to come before your people boldly.
Free from being afraid of what is ahead.
Free to talk to you as a daughter should.
Free to feel your love.
Free to walk in victory.
Free to live the best life you have designed for me.
Free to believe.
Free to dream.
Free to speak life into anything.
For the tongue is as sharp as a double-edged sword,
So, I will not speak unto this life anything that causes harm.
Free to release all hurt, pain and misery.
Free to place them at your feet.
Free to walk away and forget.
Free to smile.
Free to laugh.
Free to experience you in every way.
I am "FREE," Thank you God for "FREEDOM."

"Teach Them"

"Teach your children right from wrong and when they are grown the will still do right." Proverbs 22:6

What are we teaching our children?
Living in the future will stress you out.
Living in the past will have you depressed and anxious.
Are we teaching them things from the heart?
Are we teaching them things that should never depart?
You are living in a world of hate and hurt,
You are living in a world shattered with no goals ahead.
Whatever happened to hope?
Whatever happened to visions and dreams?
Now, I am learning it the hard way,
Instilled at a young age that Jesus is the way.
Living day by day never forgetting from whence I came.
But reassuring myself to never look back but go forward.
That is why I choose to live in the moment,
And go confidently in the direction of my dreams.
We were brought out of the darkness into the light,
For this has been a long fight
Weeping has endured for the night.
And it is His will I have in my sight.

"My Provider"

I am safe in His arms as He protects me from all harm.
I thank you Lord for all you have done.
Lord, you have been by my side thru it all,
Even mending a shattered heart.
You continue to stop and provide grace,
To a lonely and struggling race.
Never forsaken and never alone,
You are God and God alone.
Bringing in new opportunities from above.
Providing everything the enemy stole.
Joy in times of sadness,
Strength when I was weak,
Beat down by years of defeat.
Providing mercy one more time.
Provider, protector Lord you are my everything.
Father, when I needed discipline,
Mother, when I needed someone to care.
Always realizing and remembering God you are there.

"My Desert Experience"

Alone on a walk I continue to roam,
As I dream of a desert far from home.
Walking aimlessly toward the Master's plan,
As God guides my footsteps and holds my hand.
I sit up in the middle of the night and wonder,
What kind of spell am I under?
Why am I having a desert experience,
What is it that I must see?
God brought to mind the story of the dry bones.
He asked, "Can these dry bones live?"
I looked up to the sky with tears in my eyes,
Trying so hard not to cry out loud.
Praying He helps me understand the destiny,
Designed by Him for me.
A precious gift placed in my hands,
As He slowly reveals the Master's plan.
Until this assignment is completed, and His will done.
I realized that I must be the chosen one.
So, He filled me with the Holy Ghost
And said, "Speak now so they will hear."
So, people will be free from their pain and misery.
Speak a word to encourage those in bondage.
Speak to the hearts of the people so they may live.
Speak for people to understand that thru any situation,
Know that God has them in the palm of His hands.

Let them know:
Learning to trust totally in me is the only way to win.
Remind them the race is not given to the swift nor strong,
But to those who endure to the end.

Tell them:
When you have done all that you can do just stand
On the promises I have revealed.
And by Faith they are covered,
Even when it seems like the end.
God sent His Son so we could be redeemed,
Even thru the deep sands of life that tries to cover us.
And because of this they are already set free.
Watch what you do and say,
For without Him there is no other way.
His love for you will always run deep as the ocean,
And as high as the mountain can reach.
As you speak out and do my will,
You have received this desert experience.
To help these bones live.

"Healing Of The Land"

"If my own people will humbly pray and turn back to me
and stop sinning, then I will answer them from heaven.
I will forgive them and make their land fertile once again."
2 Chronicles 7:14

Living in a land of rebellion,
Sin is really running rampant.
Murder and suicide is at an all-time high.
We even have children taking their own lives.
Kids are having kids because they want someone to love.
Confusion is everywhere.
The lie has finally turned into the truth,
The enemy is trying its best to rule.
Ever since they took prayer out of school,
What are the teachers to do?
It is starting to feel like no one cares,
With this behavior we better beware.
That sin is becoming greater than the grains of sand.
How can God heal the land?
With the consequences at hand,
We need to start praying for the healing of the land.

Where can we go for the churches are closed?
And there are so many false prophets' truth be told.
What do we say, haven't you heard?
It is all written in His Word.
Take your Word and do not hesitate.
If you wait until tomorrow, it may be too late.

"Watch Your Steps"

While dealing with hurt and pain
And a whole lot of things I cannot explain.
I looked at the sky and realized this does not feel real.
To walk God's design up the mountain hill.
A path designed only for a conqueror.
A crooked path filled with rocks and boulders.
Watch your step you do not want to be bit by a rattler,
That represent all your present battles.
People that bring you past pain and discouragement,
Are determined to stomp on your confidence.
There are others watching your downward spiral into
depression.
As you seek a place for decompression.
So, throw your stones and speak your words,
Because I am covered by the one that I serve.
My God is going to impart in me,
The wisdom to endure until the end.
God is going to show up, He did in the Garden of Eden,
Will you be hiding like Adam and Eve somewhere
shivering?
This is the time that He will instill,
The tools I need to walk up the hill.

Not because I have been so right,
But for my faithfulness thru out my life.
With no worries or stress, I will always win,
You see, He gave His life for all my sins.
I will continue to make the right choices for me.
And watch how God make all things good as they
should be.

"I've Got You"

As the current took me under, I felt like I could not breathe.
Gasping, asking God, to please come rescue me.
The harder I tried to gasp for a little air,
The more the current dragged me further to nowhere.
I kicked and kicked with all my might,
And swam and swam for my dear life.
It will not be long before my air is gone,
And the blackness engulfs me, Lord, I am coming home.
I had sunk to the bottom for I had lost my hope,
Suddenly, I begin to choke.
At this moment I am losing consciousness,
And I begin to give up.
Lord, if it is my time let me go without fear,
Please settle my mind and heart and make it clear.
I heard a voice whisper my child you are not dead,
My destiny for you is up ahead.
So, close your eyes relax your mind, I will take care of you.
Instead of fighting with the current, let it push you
through.
Just like the flood I will push away the debris,
I am using this situation to push you to your victory.
Relax and play dead if that is what you want to do,
I will never leave your side, and I will bring you through.
I have been in this place before where the light begins to dim,
And all God said was "Rest in Him."

"Wisdom"

Lord, give me the wisdom:

    To be joyous during a time of misery.

Give me the wisdom:

    To believe that thru you I can achieve anything.

The wisdom:

    To love others correctly, even when they treat me bad.

The wisdom:

    To lay my burdens at your feet.

The wisdom:

    To know it is my heart that you will protect and keep.

The wisdom:

    To know that when life has me pinned to the ground,

    You are omnipresent and always around.

The wisdom to let things go.

The wisdom:

    To respond as you would and not allow emotions to take over.

The wisdom:

    To know which battles are worth fighting.

The wisdom:

    To know when to speak or just be quiet.

The wisdom:

    To walk away from anything causing me pain.

The wisdom to keep my mind focused on you.
The wisdom:
>To understand that things sometimes expire.

You are there:
When I am feeling lonely, and no one is around.
When anxiety and anger arise, it is by my side that you stand.

Because you are:
My beginning, my end, and the author of my story.

"To Love Again"

The pain I feel it should be unknown,
A pain so deep all I can do is moan.
Deep in my soul God knows the feelings I bare,
How I wish there were someone to whom I could share.
But the hurt is so deep I cannot explain,
Oh, how I wish I could love again.
Broken inside beyond repair,
As I sit around hurting and in despair.
Wishing that this pain would hurry up and leave,
But the problem is I wear my heart on my sleeve.
Wanting to wish the pain away,
Just so I can survive another day.
As life continues with anger and pain,
We take the chance to place the blame.
One way or another a promise has been broken,
And many times, ugly words have been spoken.
My soul yearns for the only thing that can repair,
The brokenness in our lives we share.
But in our minds, we just tease the situation
With more lies and intimidations.
For it is the hurt in my eyes you want to see,
But that is not the way it should be.
We blame each other for the way we feel,
And neither of us are willing to yield.

Will you continue throwing rocks and hide your hands,
Or are you willing to come together and take a stand.
Against the pain and hurt we both share
And show the world that we really care.
Whatever the course, or whatever the stress,
It is by God's love that we will pass this test.
God has promised us a better path,
It is through His joy that we will last.
No more hurt, no more brokenness, and no more pain
With Jesus in our lives, we can love each other again.

"You Lose"

To Whom This May Concern:

I am writing this letter to help you understand that I am not who people say I am or who you think I am.

I know when you think of me, you think of something bad, because now you believe the lies that others have spread. Disregarding the source, you are the one who continues to voice your opinions based on lies that someone is telling you.

I remember the times when you were down, and needed a shoulder to cry on, I was there. I remember the prayer you said you prayed in the middle of the night. I really do not know if you did or not. Everything that has been said about me you shake your head agreeing with what they say and never defending me, but you were always ready to defend someone else. Instead of trying to keep it real, you chose to step in the realm of hate, use me and tried to destroy and break my ego.

But there is something you need to know; I am not that helpless person you thought you knew. I am back and have come to my senses. I will no longer be your victim.

I refused to be used for my mind, body, or soul. I will no longer be disrespected with insults or made to feel ashamed by throwing my past in my face.

You made a choice and now it is my time to choose, your time has come to an end, and I do not want to hear from you or see you again. Satan you have loss, you cannot play or plan my life anymore. I am who God says I am, not what you have called me. You thought you had me in your trap, but God says:
I am a woman, designed by Him.
I am a child of God, covered and protected by Him.
I am not a doormat for your use, no longer will you walk all over me.

So, get lost, go on your way, every assignment has been cancelled, it is you who will fold. I know you will return but I know who you are now, and I will call you out for who you are.

In Jesus Name, I declare my Faith is in Jesus and my life is in His hands. Whatever my Father have in store for me to do, that is what I will do.

"Worship Him"

The Word of God says:
Worship Him in Spirit and in truth,
For that is what we are called to do.
Do not let His praise fall through the cracks,
Because we are too stubborn to bring worship back.
In all your mess do not fail the test,
Reach out, praise, and worship Him with your best.
For the enemy is running around town,
Bringing God's children down to the ground.
Showing you all that you can and like to do,
Without worshipping God, it is still free for you.
He is causing the believers not to believe,
And the children of God are being deceived.
We are captured by our decisions in life,
That has brought about sin and strife.
He is causing so much havoc, chaos, and pain,
It is time to bring worship back into the world again.
The bridegroom will soon choose His bride,
If you are not ready, where will you hide?
The world as we know it will be no more,
As we stand before the Father naked and poor.
Those who have passed the final test,
Our souls will have its eternal rest.
For He will soon appear, and we know not the time,
So, let us rest our souls and renew our minds.

In heaven where we are destined to be
Sitting at the feet of the one who died on calvary.
In all your ways connect to His ways,
As we worship and praise Him every day.
God has extended us much love and grace,
For one day we will be able to see Him face to face.
Look how His love lifts us up each day,
Out of all the things Satan places in our way.
You captured His heart before you were born,
It is His love that should be adorned.
One thing His love for us will never fail,
And His Word will forever prevail.
Keep the word close to your heart,
Because God said He would never depart.

"Wishing & Hoping"

How do I start?
Lost in my spirit.
Lost in my heart.
Lost in my soul.
Which way do I turn?
Trusting in no one.
Believing the lies.
Wishing and Hoping:
This was a disguise.
Dreaming of Heaven,
While living in hell.
All my dreams,
Are turning into nightmares,
All I can do is sit with a blank stare.
Hoping and Wishing:
That life was a fairy tale,
That I could click my heels
And return home.
But I have nowhere to go.
And there is no one there anymore.
Depression has got me a prisoner.
In my mind, having me wish that I were dying,
As my heart continues crying.

Hoping for an end
Wanting an end to the pain,
As I continue to stand in the rain.
Trying to understand this pain,
And all the problems I have gained.
Only to learn that love was not true,
Just a smoke screen used by you.
Satan you put on your disguise,
And now I am wise in your eyes.
You tried to cloud my mind with bad memories,
But God gave me the victory.
How do I start? Which way do I turn?
"With Jesus"

"Made Up Mind"

A wish, a dream, a touch, and a kiss.
A time of love long after being missed.
A minute, a second, an hour, a year,
Helps me to know I have nothing to fear.
Days and time flies by so fast where do it go?
No time to lose, I just keep holding on.
A memory from the past may stir up the pain,
But it feels so good to love again.
A wish, a dream, a simple touch, and a soft kiss
Makes life worth going back on that trip.
The test of survival was endurance and not strength,
It was about caring, loving and self-defense.
It is changing your mind from the way you think,
And speaking about the things that make sense.
The way you feel when chaos is everywhere,
And you feel like there is no one who really cares.
Transformation begins deep in the mind,
For anyone willing to draw the line.
To walk away from negativity all around,
And anything designed to tear you down.
The healing process must begin,
So, you will be able to love again.
The vows I stated years ago were true,
Within my heart it still yearns for you.

I did believe in love at one time,
Even when it left me broken and crying.
How long will I listen to the same sad song?
About how someone I loved did me wrong.
For this game that we call life,
Brings about a lot of hurt and strife.
God has called me to make a change,
And realize that I am carrying His name
I am in it to win it; I will not complain.
Because a lesson learned,
Is a blessing gained.
As I continue to press on in Jesus' name.
It is time to move on
That is the road I have chosen.
To see my Father up above, in all His Glory.

"Legacy"

I was not sent here to please,
I hope you will soon be on your knees.
Pushing your way through,
Thinking there is nothing to do.
Turn from your wicked ways.
For God knows the number of your days.
What is your fate, do you know the deal?
Or how much for God you did was real.
Or did you bend the truth to learn how to survive,
With your hands covering the eyes of the lies.
We decide to play hide and seek in the dark,
While our whole life is falling apart.
This is not the way God sees you,
Chunking nachos and playing peek-a-boo.
This is not a merry go ride,
Because in the end we all will die.
If you were to leave the earth today,
What would your legacy say?
Would you be known for your gentle heart?
Or would people know you because you have broken
their hearts?

Will you be known for being good or the bad?
Or someone who spoke harshly and made people sad?
Would you be the one who was misunderstood?
Or often went about bending the rules.
What will your answer be?
Heaven or Hell you will truly see,

"A Dark Way To Pursue Faith"

I looked in the well and what did I see,
Nothing but darkness staring at me.
In a place so damp and cold,
In the darkness there is no light to behold.
I felt a sense of fright and anxiety that day,
As the darkness so deep covered my way.
I asked, God, how I am supposed to move?
He said, take a step and you will see soon.
You wanted me powerless, I cannot see,
Just what you have in store for me.
God said, it is not by sight, do you believe?
That every step you take has been ordained by me.
The path is dark there are things you do not need to see,
Until then just believe.
If you keep walking you will soon see the path,
Stay focused, look, you are on the right track.
Trust and believe that whatever concerns you, concerns me.
That is why you must go down on bended knees.

I know your path and you will not be deceived.
For I will hold back the arrows of the enemy.
This is not the time to worry or turn around,
Victory is ahead if you remain grounded.
Keep on stepping and make your own history,
Because your Faith will lead you to victory.

"Which Game Are You Playing?"

The enemy wants to take me out,
But that is not what it is all about.
This has been a continuous fight,
You and me and knowing what is right.
Russian roulette you pointed at my head,
Wishing I was already dead.
But I will not go out like this,
Let us continue with some of your tricks.
To me this is a game of chess,
Strategically being placed by the best.
Under God's amazing grace,
I take my chance because of my Faith.
Checkers could be the game,
Oh, no, you must crown me again.
A game of tug-of-war may erupt,
I may fall but I will get back up.
For every battle is a struggle,
But that is okay God's got me covered.
Red moves, red moves send your minions my way,
For once they cross this line, they are here to stay.
One, two, three, red light, STOP!!
My God is already at the top.

Red Rover, red rover, I dare you to come over,
What an invitation in time to discover,
That my mind is what you keep coming for,
And I am here to tell you, I will not take it anymore.
Mind over matter and I am beginning to win,
For it belongs to God and it is His until the very end.
I am tired of playing your games
I am casting you down in Jesus' name.
No, you cannot have my soul
Because it is under God's control.
God said, He will supply all my needs,
And keep me safe until it is my time to leave,
So, stop pulling on my sleeve.
Because I know you are the enemy.
My God has already spit you out,
And sent you to hell without a doubt.
Take your games, and tricks and start your sail,
Back to the pits of hell where nothing prevails.

"Planted For A Purpose"

At this moment I am a planted seed
Ready for God to provide me what I need.
Waiting to burst up thru the moist soil,
To show the beauty of the Lord.
To complete the work, He has placed inside of me,
To show all His grace and mercy.
It may seem like a dark place down here,
But remember God is always near.
To see the enemy trying to sneak in,
Let us know that they will not win.
Coming into the camp to cause defeat,
Which is not an option if you believe.
For it is not in my God's plans
To stay here stuck below the ground.
Against the very thing set up to destroy me
That is not what is predestined to be.
A prick in my side as a thorn snips the shin,
Gave me the strength to know it is not the end.
An open wound oozing into a life no longer bound,
I am so glad it was Jesus that I found.
Jesus has already claimed His crown,
And with Him I am heaven bound.
An ultimate death we all shall see,
For predestined lives are set for you and me.
But through God's grace we shall abound,
Because my God is always around.

"From Now Until Eternity"

From the top of the mountain,
I will sing your praise.
I will continue to glorify your name.
When the world seems against me and I feel alone,
It is your name "Jesus" that I will call.
I will continue to put my trust in you,
I know you will bring me thru.
Renew my mind.
Repair my soul.
Transform me from the past.
I will continue to lift your name,
Your name is first and will always be the same.
One day will come and I will be gone,
Gone to my heavenly home.
From depression, anxiety, and misery,
A world full of selfishness and envy.
And a place they say is the land of plenty.
No more fake friends, fake love, and fake alibi's,
No more wondering as I look up at the sky.
No more tears left for me to cry,
No long time to say goodbye.

Alas, at home in my Father's arms,
Away from earthly hurt or harm.
All I have seen is jealousy and hate,
As I live my life and continue to wait.
Do not cry for me for I am finally free,
I have no chains holding me.
Until then I will be an instrument for Him to use,
Until it is my number that He should choose.

"Be Still"

"Be still and know that I am God." Psalms 46:10

Searching for a sign that you are still here,
For it is your presence I seek.
Seeking a place to find peace of mind.
Searching for myself, I have not seen me in a while.
Feeling lost and losing sleep,
As I watch the world crumble at my feet.
Yet I still find myself alone,
With no one to talk to and nowhere to go.
Alone by myself, trying not to give up,
Searching for someone I can just touch.
I am stirring around in the wrong mix,
By searching for a worldly fix.
Still trying to handle everyday life,
While struggling with insecurities deep inside.
You have allowed the enemy to get in
And he surely does not want you to win.
Those memories buried inside your mind,
Are things that have bothered you years at a time.
A broken spirit, and a crushed heart are reminders of pain,
And constantly speaking negative about your name.
Like a mural on the wall, you begin to fade away,
Into the chaos and confusion, of that day.

Alone in your tears surrounded by pain,
Crying because you cannot take it again.
You cannot handle this, I heard the enemy say,
All because I am standing in your way.
The more I whispered in your ear,
You stood and shuttered in fear.
That is why I am getting in your head.
Because you think I want you dead.
Unequipped to fight that is your will,
But God is telling you be still.
I will give you the wisdom to endure,
And for this remember my promises are sure.
The will is stand and not fight,
But to do those things that are right.
Your victory has already been won,
If you keep your eyes on the son.
Say yes and obey His will,
And do what the Master said, "Be Still."

"My Testimony"

Today is an incredibly special day,
Two years ago, I was ready to take my life away.
Tired of worrying, stressed beyond compare,
It did not seem like no one cared.
I was lost in myself did not know how to change,
Sometimes not sure of my real name.
I was afraid to take a step for the fear of failure,
Could not let go of the past for I felt that would be forever.
Previous pain was keeping me from growing,
While all the time your true self has been showing.
Anxiety inside had me dreading the day
Not really knowing what to say.
Negative thoughts racing through my head,
Wanting to stay right there in the bed.
Wishing I knew how I could get ahead.
And not knowing in which direction I could be lead.
I opened my eyes a prisoner in my mind,
As I continued to remember the past times.
Searching for a way to fight,
Things I could not understand kept me uptight.
When I heard a voice say, "I have your hand."
Lean on me and I will help you understand.

So, it was my life God decided to spare,
It is because of Him that I am even able to care.
For your treasure lies in your heart,
And you will never reach it if you do not start.
Look deep inside and fear will subside
Step out on Faith and enjoy the ride
Your forever life began today,
Do not be afraid because I will lead the way.

"Struggling"

I sit back and wonder how our lives can be filled with so much hate and misery. When this is not the way God created us to be. Bogged down with depression and anxiety. Afraid to let things go that keeps reminding each of us of how it is truly not in God we trust. For the people in the world has lost sight of the difference between right and wrong. As we remain in the same place and not moving ahead. But many wishing they were dead. Playing the game, keeping secrets, placing the blame, yet we wonder why in the middle of the night we cry. When the sun comes up in the morning we are stuck in the same place. Even as God extends us grace. Yet we play the same game hoping we do not go insane. Trying to be who we are not supposed to be. I thought things were getting better, but they seem to be getting worse. I thought that the sun would shine, but it looks like clouds all the time. Take a step back and you will see, so many causes of our miseries: family ties, generational curses, keeps us arguing fussing and fighting, without a purpose and without an end. Afraid to be wrong always want to be right, that is all I have is a struggle and fight, eager to win and determined not to lose. Proving yourself is the only thing on your mind. But that is not what God wants during this time.

Take me to a place, I have not seen, a place that I will see in my dreams. A place where I can be free, to be who you God have called me to be. Lord, I want to be in the place you have designed for me, behind the veil where everything is true. Bring about the change you want to be and make your dream a reality.

"Stop Crying, Hold On"

I heard a voice inside saying my child stop crying,
For time is almost here.
You have fought your fight and joy is almost near.
Keep the faith; do not give up,
For I have predestined victory on your end.
As you walk through your storms,
The poems that you write speaks to the heart of
women and men.
And they are poems around the actual pain,
And feelings you may feel.
Your stories bring about a since of relief,
To release the burdens from your heart.
Remember the pain and keep pressing on,
For your victory is not far off.
Keep your eyes on me and you will see,
The promises that I have for thee.
Remember even though your victory is near,
Another storm may be brewing my friend.
As I began to write again,
A lot of thoughts go through my mind.
Wondering the what if's and why is of life
Is it my time to die?
As I think back to that day on calvary,
As I see in my mind the blood dripping down

Barely missing Jesus eyes,
From the crown of thorns, they placed on His head.
The pain in my heart compared to what they used
To pierce his side.
As the blood flowed down and
As they cast lots on the ground
Not caring about the sin.
What if Jesus did not do it?
What would my life be like?
My heart hurts, I just want to cry.
My heart is pumping as if it will jump out of my chest.
But I heard His voice say, "Stop Crying."
Let the word of God sink in as your Season begin.
Hold on to the instructions I have given to you,
Your promises will begin to shine through.
You have been fighting a long time,
It is your time to rise and take your place.
I have provided grace to pull you through.
Faith has gone ahead to bless you.

"Memories Of A Lost Love"

I woke up with you on my mind,
Hoping our love would pass the test of time.
Memories deep in my heart
Of the very first day we met, and I start,
To wonder how a man like you were here,
Always hoping you would stay near.
But as life goes on,
I guess the feelings are gone.
I remember how it felt when we first met,
Nothing but excitement,
Ready to see each other again,
Hoping the night would never end.
What is this I cannot explain,
The reason I smile when I hear your name.
But the day came when all of that was gone
And now we sit all alone.
Wondering where we went wrong
That is the reason for this song.
A memory of a love so strong
Has turned into a faded memory and a broken heart.
With a broken heart seeing you call,
Really make me forget it all.

The way it feels to be let down
Alone by myself with no one around.
And you have decided to move ahead with your life
Leaving me with heartache and strife.
My heart is saying no I cannot take this hurt anymore
But you act like you can just move on.
Like the love we had was never real.
Just something that you did not feel.
Like I deserve to be here alone,
While you let your life continue to go on.
But I will one day love again,
Until then be well my friend.

"Why Me"

King & Queen readjust your crown
In this season you will not drown.
Put a smile on your face, and lift your chin,
That is the only way that you will win.
Why are you looking down toward the ground?
Looking for an answer that cannot be found.
Why are you listening to everyone that told you a lie?
Start looking up towards the sky.
Why are you feeling miserable and blue?
And not caring to hear the truth.
If in God, you have put your trust.
Your worries will never overtake you,
There are times you must try,
Even if things do not look right.
You are amazing can't you see,
But because of past mistakes you always disagree.
Start looking to the hills the only help you know.
Pray and meditate, God has it all under control.
For God has not given you a spirit of fear,
So, rejoice now for your breakthrough is near.
Believe in times of trouble,
Everything will turn out alright.
Have Faith,

You have already won the victory.
The day is still young,
There is plenty of work to be done.
A helping hand is needed.
Souls need to be saved.
Love to be shared.
Chains broken.
Now, King and Queen adjust your crown.
There is still plenty of work to be done all around.

"I Said" but "God Said"

I SAID:

I have been in the valley way to long,
I heard a voice whispering my child come home.
I see the mountains before me,
Wondering how this can be.
I want to leave but this mountain is so tall,
If I climb it I might slip and fall.
I stared at the problem before me,
I realize that it is blocking my destiny.
Oh, but they forgot who we are,
We are not quitters we have come to far.
In my mind we will figure out a plan
To get where God wants us, not worrying about man.
As God begins to elevate us as He chooses
This stumbling block to shall be moved.

GOD SAID:

You have been down too long, and the time has come,
For those dry bones to come alive.
But I need you here so that you can get your mind right.
You have given your best and given your heart.
You have loved hard and carried my heart.

Now take the time and embrace my love.
As I elevate you like never before.
Be still and know I have the plans for your future.
Wait on me and you will soon see,
The reason why I have chosen thee.
Rest and know you will continue to grow.
Continue to trust, your faith will keep you close
To me and everything you need.
Believe and let me lead.
I have ordered your steps and ordained your path.
I will open doors that no man can see,
And keep you covered and safe for eternity.

"Watch And Pray"

My heart broke in two when you walked out the door,
Deep in my heart I knew I could not take it anymore.
But I remembered a scripture that said,
For we wrestle not against flesh and blood
But against powers we cannot see.
That was enough for me to believe,
God can turn any situation around.
As long as I have faith and keep him around,
Your time will eventually come to an end.
I need to talk to you and let you know,
The world is coming to an end.
Open your eyes and see,
We are living in the time of the antichrist.
Destroying everything that we have held dear.
Families are being broken,
Hearts are hurting.
People are being disrespected.
Selfish ambitions.
Jealousy Spirit.
Coming against the flesh stronger than before.
Many rumors of war, spreading across the world.
As famine spreads around the land.
The time will come, and we will soon see,
That we have no choice but to go down on bended knee.

For God is surely not pleased with what He sees.
He sent His Son to Calvary, for all of our sins.
Now, He is saying, "Call my children home."
Will you be going, or will you be left behind?
Left here without your loved ones all alone?
Left with a broken heart as the Lord goes out the door.
With nowhere to go and nowhere to hide.

"Broken"

I tried Lord, but somehow, I missed the mark,
Now I am sitting here with a broken heart.
I was faithful and loyal until the end,
But I guess this was all pretend.
The love I thought was going to be true,
Ended up with me having a heart that is blue.
From all the things that we have been through
I wish I could see the wrong path that I chose.
That turned this love into something that can be dissolved.
I am remembering how things use to be.
While you are trying to figure out the mystery where you
belong. Who's side you want to be on.
Which side of the track you will choose?
Or whether you win or lose.
I thought of you,
But could not remember the last time you spoke to me.
While you are struggling with your own reality,
And with my heart broken, I will press on my way,
Even when I cannot fix myself to pray.
With my heart broken, I will forgive you,
For it is God's love that heals inside.
Wounded and bruised again, I say,
Lord, I honestly believe that love was sent from above.
But it is hard to ever believe again.
In true love lasting until the end.

"Choices"

My soul is worn
And I do not feel whole.
I do not think I can take anymore.
My heart barely beats,
And the smile on my face I try to keep.
Down on my luck,
Feeling like I am stuck.
I cannot go to the left nor to the right,
As my mind continues to wander through the night.
Restless and stressed hoping for the best
That things would change, and I get some rest.
Beat down to the spirit; okay you win,
All I want to do is find a hole I can crawl in.
If I do, I lose; If I do not, I lose,
So which option do I choose?
Right is right, wrong is wrong,
My heart is broken, I give it all,
And still, I feel like I will fall.
But my time is not God's time to be,
And I cannot see, all that He is planning for me.
You took away my voice, so, I write instead
That is how I gained strength, in what you have said.
There is a glimmer of light in the dark room.
A hug of love will pull you thru.

A hopeless vision with life secure.
A smile of gratitude to let you know,
A shoulder you can lean on forevermore.
I feel the pain you are going thru,
So, do not forget I am holding you.
For the world to see the real me
I am Christ and I give you the victory.
Keep on pushing and remember I promised you
That no matter what I will see you thru.

"Willing"

Take a minute to walk in my shoes,
And I will sit back and allow you to.
Take the pain that was created to drain me,
And let me know if I will ever be free.
Accept a mission designed for you,
As you wonder if the message is true.
Will you begin to speak?
Or will you accept defeat?
Will you speak life into dry bones?
That have sat so long they have nowhere to go.
Battle sore, and soft they may not be able to stand,
So, take the time to reach out and take their hand.
Stop the tears from falling from my eyes,
And let your Spirit continue to abide.
Lord, chase away all my fears,
Speak through me to make it clear.
Make my heart beat again.
With the love you have imparted within,
It is not I the people need to see,
But it is your glory that they need to trust and believe.
God is telling us to speak,
And not accept a life of defeat.
Which path will you choose?
Which place will you dwell?

Where are you willing to stand?
Will it be among the living or the dead?
Are you willing to pray until something happens?
Are you willing to do what needs to be done?
Until your race on this earth you have won.
For me, I will dwell in the temple,
Until you alone release me.
Whatever path you choose, I know that you will keep me.
Until then speak to my soul and direct my feet
To the people you have chosen for me to speak.

A- Anxious
    N- Nervous
        X- X-Ray
        Irritable
        E- Envy
            T- Tired
            Y- Yield

There is an overcast cloud in your life,
A cloud that causes so much strife.
Anxiety is its name,
And it does not care whose life it claims.
You are addicted to the pain in your life
That continues to bring you stress and strife.
Hoping you do not lose your mind,
Because of friends, lies and alibis.
Anxiety is at an all-time high,
Challenging you to live or die.

Playing with the thoughts in your mind,
Making it hard for you to decide.
Like a mural on a wall, you fade away,
Into a life of anxiety, you cave.
Anxiety sets in at the thought of losing a friend
Ashamed, bewildered, and hurting within.
Broken hearted, and a weary soul,
You are feeling down, Lord I need a place to go.
Where did I go wrong?
What makes my heart mourn?
Self-doubt will bring you back to the storm,
Feeling like you cannot go on.
Break loose from this curse and set yourself free,
From a life of anxiety, chaos, and total misery.
Reach out for something out of sight,
Have faith and believe it will be alright.
Revive your Spirit as God said you should,
And you will reach that goal you thought you never would.
There is a greatness inside of you,
Make anxiety mad and trust God to see you through.
So do not let ANXIETY cloud your day
But let Jesus show you the way.

"Where Do You Stand"

Spiritual wickedness is invading the land.
And it has you wondering where do you stand?
Constant change everywhere you turn.
Hoping one day we will all soon learn.
That God is not pleased with the way things are going today.
Lost in a web of deceit,
Looking at nothing but defeat.
Murders are happening everywhere.
No one ever seems to care.
Family and friends fighting each other,
We need to take cover.
Like Adam and Eve in the Garden of Eden,
He will come back walking, and He knows what is needed.
God is calling your name.
Stop, watch, and listen to what He proclaims.
I am here for you, trust me for I have brought you through.
I brought you to a place you have never been before.
A place you have never seen before.
A place in your dreams you adored.
A realm you have never been on before.
A safe place from all hurt and harm.
A place you can enjoy the table prepared for you.
A place free from pain in your soul.
From secrets kept in your heart to hold.
Abused and accused of many lies.

That has kept you feeling trapped on the inside.
A place ready to release all negativity.
This is a test of your longevity.
Will you praise or will you fold?
Under the pressure of what is being told?
Destruction is going to begin in the land.
So, where will you stand?

"Love Out Of Bounds"

Where did our love go?
How could we lose interest?
How could we just walk away?
When we made a promise to God to stay,
And never let our love stray.
Our love can pass the test of time,
If only we make up our mind.
The vows that we made before God and friends,
We knew then our love would never end.
For once our hearts used to beat as one.
But a storm has come in and it has won.
For better or worse that's what we said,
Until God calls or both of us are dead.
Rich or poor, sickness and in health,
Working each day because there was no wealth
What could have caused us to change our words?
Was it mistrust or something that you heard?
We were trying to be safe from all the vultures on our back,
Just waiting for our downfall and our season of lack.
My crown has tilted, and it just might fall,
But I'll keep my head up in spite of it all.
Keeping tabs on our flaws will keep you confused
As you sit alone in the corner making up new rules.
You're the first one to say that you object

And the last one to say what you won't accept.
To looking for love with all your heart
But having the nerve to say we need to part.
A problem not faced, and two hearts broken,
Missing the mark of words not spoken.
I'm wondering if we will ever be content,
Apart or together that's the whole extent.
The light deep inside for you no longer glow,
And to be with you would only be a show.

I'm going to stand right in this place
For you are no longer welcomed in our space.
So, I need you to turn and walk away
Take your things you just can't stay.
It's over now and we are through,
But remember one thing "I'll always love you."

"Give Hope A Chance"

When God had me in mind,
He created the sun to shine.
From the East to the West
Internationally known to do my best.
From the North to the South,
It is time to stop and talk about,
How to turn away from worry and pain
And give HOPE a chance to rise again.
It is the tongue that keeps tearing your life apart,
From the selfishness deep in your heart.
As negative thoughts run through your mind.
It causes your light to be dim all the time.
A decision you made under wrong intentions,
Is nothing but evil thoughts and manipulation.
Like a mural on the wall, you soon fade away,
Into the chaos and confusion, that you gave.
What is a dream without a vision?
What is a vision without hope?
What is life without God?
Defeat is not an option, it is not in God's plans
So, learn to pray and take hold to God's hands.
A gentle word spoken can easily turn away,
The hurtful things that people can say.

Mustard Seed Faith is what we need,
To walk in life and yes, succeeded.
To reconnect with the true love of my life.
I'm reaching out to my life, JESUS CHRIST!
He called my name, came, and rescued me,
And said, "forever in life walk in your destiny."

"Trick Or Treat"

Trick: The enemy
Getting people with fakeness from the start,
Doing good, and really know how to play the part.
Love so fake it really looked real,
It is unable to detect just how you feel.
The Mask is on, and you are coming in disguise,
Tricking people to believe that God is inside.
Sneaking in like a thief in the night,
Not to revive or help but ready to fight.
You are ready to begin your evil plan to destroy,
Everything, and everyone we have always adored.
With a look of disgust in your eyes,
You keep trying to find how to get inside.
Not thinking twice of who you encounter
Only about who you can hinder.
Wishing and hoping your disguise will not be revealed,
And hoping that the lies you told will always be concealed.
Continuing to bring about doubt and fear,
While stoking the flames every day of the year.
He brings about hate and a lot of confusion,
And sit back and laugh and think it is amusing.
Oh, the tricks that he will play
So, you can have a bad day.

Treat: God's plans

For every trick there is a reason,
And the truth is in God because it is His season.
The treats you receive are part of His plan,
So that we can live free in this land.
You may have everyone believing you are it,
But there is one thing you should never forget.
The Word of God has made it plain,
And all we must do is call on His name.

We may forget it for just a minute.
The Word of God has a lot of treats in it.

God said:

No weapon form against me shall prosper.
I will supply all your needs.
Love is the greatest gift of all.
Faith is the substance of things hoped for the evidence
of things not seen.
Draw nigh to God and He will draw nigh to you.
Come unto me all that labor, I will give you rest.
I will never leave you nor forsake you.
I know the plans I have for you.

The Word can go on forever as our attack,
And stop Satan in his tracks.
Believe in what God said He will do,
And he will forever cover you.

"God's Hands"

Every day I speak with you,
You give me strength to believe,
Anything I hoped for, I can still achieve.
A time in space you have designed,
Saying don't worry about those you left behind.
You have ignited my heart to wonder,
Just what you have in store.
For God can turn back the hands of time,
And in my life give me more.
You give me hope for the future,
How much more can I endure?
When I have a God that will restore,
Where I have missed the mark so many times before.
For many will not understand what is going on
But God wants you alone.
To pull you from all dramas, and pain,
And get you to trust in Him again.
As your emotions began to rise.
He will hold you until they subside.
My heart skips a beat whenever I hear your name,
For all the love you gave me thru heartaches and pain.
God is carrying you to a special place,
To provide you with rest and His marvelous grace.
But there is one thing you should not forget,
That you were the one that delayed the process.

"Alone But Not Alone"

Alone in the valley so dark and cold,
I'm reaching out for something that I can hold.
Complete darkness all around, I must feel my way,
What is this I'm stepping on; this is not my day.
Grossly things under my feet, I can't explain
Crawling, grabbing at each step, all I feel is pain.
As I stepped on them, they begin to multiply,
And tears begin to roll out of my eyes.
I looked down and much to my surprise,
It was fake love, fake friends, fake family grabbing at my side.
In my mind I was trying to reason,
Why the constant betrayal and treason?
This is what I am talking about,
The ones that hide until the lights goes out.
The pain of finding out that you were not true
Have left me standing, wondering who are you?
You're so busy trying to figure out my sins,
When you need to stop feeding the demon within.
With the tongue of a serpent, you hissed my name,
But you and I are not the same.
Down in this valley so dark and cold,
Looking for that light that I can behold.
There's a light in the distance that I see
Beckoning, whispering come follow me.

I hear the voice of my Father saying
"My sheep knows my voice and I know them."
And it's not your path I follow,
But my Father who sent me.
My God has the recordings of all the times,
That I have ever crossed the line.
The secret life you thought I tried to hide
Turned out to be nothing but a pack of lies.
Just like Judas, he knew what he had done
You seek out gossip just for fun.
I see the light and I'm walking forward
And leave you here, that is your choice.
Others may believe that there is no good in me,
Compare it to the person you pretend to be.
So, go on and scandalize my name.
Because I am claiming victory in Jesus' name.

"There's No Place Like Home"

As I head down life's highway,
On such a beautiful day.
No place to call home,
In my mind I will continue to roam.
Until I find the place where I can feel free
From carrying around all this misery.
As I look up at the sky,
Thinking about how many tears I've cried.
Trying to keep myself sane.
As people cause unnecessary hurt and pain.
They are trying hard to destroy my mind,
By reminding me of thoughts I've left behind.
Hoping that I can't take anymore,
Of a broken spirit and a soul full of holes.
While on this battlefield constantly sharing,
I wonder is anyone really caring.
Sometimes I feel alone sitting on the shelf,
With a sense of doubt in myself.
You may come and mess with my head,
With the thoughts of negativity and lies instead.
But all the world is in a state of confusion
Transitioning from life to a time of decisions.

Uncertainties, sickness, heartache, and disease,
Has brought many people to their knees.
Broken promises are all you speak about
It is time for you to seek God out.
He is the one who knows all about you
The only one that can carry you through.
He will provide you a place of rest,
A place where you can give Him your best.
I' m still heading down the highway,
On this beautiful day.
Praying that God will continue to light the way,
So, that all His children will have a blessed day.

"Thoughts For The Soul"

There are times when we ask God for something and God provides it, but sometimes we complain because it's not what we really wanted. Despite your decision, He said He would supply your needs. Stop complaining and start praising.

Some days the pain is more than you can bear. Some days it feels like you can't find any peace. Some days you just want to give up. Some days it seems like prayer doesn't work. Remember- Jesus said, "He will never leave you nor forsake you." He will be there for you, look to Jesus. He will change your midnight experience into daylight.

When you're feeling all alone and again it feels like there is no one to call. Fear is beginning to set in and you do not understand. You're in need of a friend and you don't know what to do call on Jesus and He will come to you.

God will give you peace that surpasses all understand. He will hold you close, wipe your tears away, forgive you with a forgiving heart, and love you with forever love inspite of all you have done in your lifetime. Look to the hills because your help comes from above.

For me to think and live is Christ inside of me. Through drugs, alcohol, abuse, indecisions, suicide, and pain. Through everything I have been through you brought me out. Thank you, Lord, for your protection and love for me.

God has a plan for your life, a place for you to be. A friend that will stand by you, with an ear to listen, and words of encouragement to you. Don't let doubt, dictate your path, trust the path maker Jesus Christ

Hurt, pain, heartache, stress, depression, anxiety, hatred, and unforgiving are all part of Satan's trap to bring you down and feel alone.
Step out and STEP into Love, Joy, Peace, Patients, Gentleness, Goodness, Faith, Meekness and Self-Control, these are the things that will bring you happiness, and joy.

Take the time to sit quietly, and listen to a song, listen to the words, let the song take over your heart, mind and soul. Take that time to worship and praise God for all He has done for you that day and all that He plan to do, and the activities of the day will drift away.

Pray when you want to, pray when you do not want to, pray when things happen in your life, pray when your life is going haywire. Prayer is the soul sincere desire to tell God what you want and how you feel. PRAY…. PRAY…. PRAY…. God wants to hear your voice.

You gave me hope—when I was afraid to hope.
You gave me peace—when I felt so confused.
You gave me Love—when I thought no one cared.
You gave me understanding—when I could not comprehend.
You held my hand- and told me not to let go.
You wiped my tears away- and said for each one I would
be blessed.
You held me up—when I felt like I would fall.
I wanted to give up—and you said hold on, do not give up.
You said come unto me all that are heavy laden, and I
will give you rest. —I said, "I give my life to you and
surrender my all.

Made in the USA
Columbia, SC
12 December 2024

47970186R00054